WHOOPI
GOLDBERG

BOOK

AVON BOOKS  NEW YORK

AVON BOOKS, INC.
1350 Avenue of the Americas
New York, New York 10019

Copyright © 1997 by Whoopi Goldberg
Cover photo by Mark Seliger/Outline
Published by arrangement with William Morrow and Company, Inc.
Visit our website at **http://www.AvonBooks.com**
ISBN: 0-380-72979-2

First Avon Books Printing: October 1998

AVON TRADEMARK REG. U.S. PAT. OFF. AND IN OTHER COUNTRIES, MARCA
REGISTRADA, HECHO EN U.S.A.

Printed in the U.S.A.

WCD   10   9   8   7   6   5   4   3   2   1

To Frank; my daughter, Alex;
my brother, Clyde; and my mom, Emma . . .
the soup from which this all flows

A grateful nod to Tommy, assistant extraordinaire; Dan Strone, agent extraordinaire; and Rob Weisbach, editor extraordinaire, who kept saying, "Would'ya? Could'ya? Don'tcha?" Well, I would, I could, I do . . . and I did. Thanks.

RIFFS

It's not what you call me, but what I answer to.

—African proverb

BOOK

FATE

At birth, I knew something was coming. As soon as I popped into the birth room, I looked over in a corner, and there was my old man Destiny smilin' at me.

My mother knew too. She felt I was gonna be special. Different. From the very beginning, she knew. The story she tells is that I came out—headfirst, of course—pulled one arm through, looked around the delivery room, turned to the light, put my thumb in my mouth, and stared right back at all the folks who were staring at me. The spotlight was on me for the very first time, and I guess I thought it was kinda cool. Hey, what's not to like?

I supposedly stayed that way for a while, in my serious, don't-mess-with-me pose; and from the way everyone was fussing, you'd think I'd taken a bow, or told a joke or something. The nurses and doctors started bringing in all the other nurses and doctors for a look. They'd never seen a kid make such an entrance, with such an attitude. They were coming in from all over, just to see.

Right then, I knew my life was gonna be different. Now I don't mean to leave the impression that I knew *exactly* what was ahead, 'cause it wasn't that way at all. I mean, I was a baby, right? A newborn. But I carried that moment with me to where I just figured I'd get a job, make some money, maybe leave my mark before I was through. I popped out knowing everything'd be fine.

And then some startling shit happened. I started thinking.

TRUST

I don't care how many people our presidents have slept with. I truly don't. It doesn't take away from who they are or what they're about or what they might accomplish. Just because a guy gets his tip wet once in a while, it doesn't make him a bad president. It doesn't even make him a bad guy. It's just part of the human package.

Take John Kennedy—this young, good-looking guy who believed that everyone was created equal and that you could do things within your reach, within your sphere, and make the world a better place. This notion, that we could all make a difference, flowed from JFK into our schools and our neighborhoods. It didn't matter that he was fucking Mari-

Whoopi
Goldberg

lyn Monroe. It mattered that he got us thinking in this civic-minded way. What mattered was that he had us believing we mattered. It's a dusty sentiment from a long time ago, but for me it came from folks like Kennedy and Martin Luther King and Medgar Evers, and it has stayed with me, no matter what shit journalists and historians have been digging up on any of these guys. The scandals might be titillating, but they're just not relevant.

It's the same today. Take any politician from my generation and ask them how many people they've slept with, or what kinds of drugs they've ingested, or where they stood on Vietnam, and you know you're bound to piss off someone with the answer. The people who smoked dope, the people who didn't . . . You can't be all things to all people, and you're fucked if you try.

Look, for all we know, the prez is a great husband. We don't know what goes on in a marriage, but we do know that being married doesn't mean you will never fuck up. We all fuck up. Presidents just fuck up on a public stage. Has this president made some mistakes in his marriage? Maybe. But what president hasn't? Eisenhower? Roosevelt? A lot of these cats we now think of as great presidents were getting a little something on the side, but it didn't make them any less

8

presidential. It just came with the ter-
ritory.

Did Bill Clinton, as governor, come
on to Paula Jones? We'll never know
for sure, but we can think it through. This man
was the governor of Arkansas. Come on, it
would have been pretty stupid if he did. But,
okay, even smart people do stupid things.
Maybe he did make a play for her, and she
wasn't into it. Maybe she was into it and then
pulled back. Or maybe it didn't happen at all.
Who knows? I just can't imagine that he took
his penis out and waved it at her. *That's* something you'd holler about right away. You know,
if you're concerned about the man's ethics and
the moral fiber of this country, then you go out
right away and say, "The governor of this state
just pulled his penis out and waved it at me
and I want to stop him from ever doing it
again." That's the time to do it.

I felt the same way about Anita Hill and
Clarence Thomas. If things went down like
Anita Hill said they went down, then why
leave the asshole on the job to keep harassing
other women? File the complaint. You don't
wait five years and expect to be taken seriously.
I'm sorry, you just don't.

But that shit doesn't matter, because ultimately what happened, or didn't, is
between Bill Clinton and Paula Jones. The
president will have to deal with his own

Whoopi Goldberg

mess, and it's none of our fucking business. I don't care if he boned a sheep, if that's his thing. Some people like sheep. I've never tried one, so I can't say whether or not this is a good thing, but where a president puts his penis has nothing to do with the work he did in Arkansas or New York or Kennebunkport or Boston, or what he can still do in Washington. I can't look at this man and say, "You, because you came on to this woman and showed her your weenie, you are not equipped to make decisions on my behalf." That's crap. Shit like this happens every day. Decisions are being made by passionate people doing things in their personal lives that I would not do in mine. Are they bad guys? I don't think so. Maybe they're just misguided, or misinformed, or horny.

Look, men in power get laid. They do. And when pussy calls there are a lot of men who respond. Men do that. Sadly, the inverse hardly ever happens, at least not to me. Power makes women masculine in the eyes of most men. This is what I've been told. That's why people get so pissed off at Hillary Clinton. They think, Well, you know, she just wants to be him. I think, No, she knows what the fuck she's doing, she's all right. But people don't want to hear it because power and sexuality in women does not compute. Men don't throw themselves at you. They want to

take the lead. That's the way they've
been brought up, and women have
been brought up to play into that. I'm
sorry, but we have. It's why Marcia
Clark can bust her butt, on a public servant's
salary, and still be second-guessed because she
had to put her kids in day care in order to go to
work. Guys don't have to put up with that shit;
they're expected to work their butts off. But
when a woman does it, she has to apologize for
neglecting her children.

There's a huge double standard. It's not just
about sex, it's about everything, and when it
starts to fuck up our politics it gets me pissed
off. We've allowed our two-party system to
become about cutting the other guy off at the
knees, and the easiest way to do that is to dig
up some dirt on your opponent. This is what
passes for debate in a modern democracy:
"Yeah, maybe I have cheated on my wife, but
you have a thing for transsexuals." This is what
we've become, and in a relatively short space
of time.

Until Watergate, we never really paid much
attention to what went on behind closed doors
in Washington. Office doors, bedroom doors,
we just didn't want to know. But then, suddenly, we looked Richard Nixon in the face and
saw ourselves. It was a traumatic thing.
Nixon was the full catastrophe, but he was
real and tangible and human. And the 11

people thought, This is just too much. So we started looking for leaders who were infallible, thinking we would someday hit on the right guy. Gerald Ford was a decent guy, with a great wife and shaky legs, but he was too ordinary. Jimmy Carter was wholesome and sincere and different, and he had his own good woman at his side, but then he went and "lusted in his heart" in a *Playboy* interview. (Who the hell lusts in his heart? Go out and lust in the haystack, or the peanut shed, or wherever a good old farm boy is meant to do his lusting. And don't go tellin' *Playboy* about it when you're through.)

For a while Ronald Reagan had us thinking he was the savior. Or maybe folks just had themselves convinced he'd ride in on his white horse and clean out the mess and fight back the bad guys and leave us all in peace and prosperity. No one asked if he was getting any extra nooky on the side, because no one cared.

By the time we reached George Bush and his thousand points of light, we didn't think to ask about *his* extramarital affairs. We ran Gary Hart out of town 'cause he turned up on a boat in Bimini with Donna Rice, but we seemed to hold George Bush to a different standard. Did we crucify Gary Hart because of his transgression, or because of the manner of his transgression? If it was the latter, man, we

gave this guy a raw deal. Somebody
took Gary Hart's picture on a boat
and sold it to the tabloids. I understand how that happens. Does it
mean he was boning this woman in the middle
of a campaign? Maybe, maybe not. But with
Bush, it was considered unseemly to even
bring it up, and then this lady surfaced and
started crowing about how she'd been sleeping
with him for years, which in itself is kinda
scary. But it didn't matter. We liked George
enough to let this one slide, and we liked Barbara a whole lot more and were not about to
dignify the allegations with our suspicions,
because, you know, we didn't want to upset
her any more than the situation already had.

With Clinton, the character debate wasn't
only about his sex life. It was about Vietnam,
and dope, and his ability to shift with the tides.
It was about this young guy who didn't fight in
his generation's war, or inhale his generation's
dope. Forget that he thought Vietnam was an
unjust war, as we can all now pretty much
agree. Forget that. He didn't do like everyone
else. He didn't do like his opponents. They
were there. "We saved the world," they said,
but they made it seem that Clinton's actions
stood for something more than a generational
difference in thinking. There was no dis-
cussion about the ethics of a whole generation—mine, and Clinton's—because our

ethics weren't the ethics of George Bush and Bob Dole. The Republicans talked a lot about going to Vietnam and fighting for the "right thing," but to some of us it was a little vague what that right thing actually was.

I just kicked back and looked at the whole thing as a big old poop pile, and by now it's gotten to where we will never find another candidate from either party who's gonna come up smelling like a rose unless he's been in a box his entire life. And who wants a candidate who's been in a box his entire life? We've all done stuff we wish we hadn't, said things we wish we could just suck back in our faces and leave unsaid, taken positions that no longer reflect our views. Does that negate what we're doing now? No way.

Bill Clinton could be a great president. He knows what he's done, and he knows what he's doing. Judge him on what he does in office, as president. Should politicians be held to a higher standard of behavior than the rest of us? Absolutely, but we need to be realistic, and we need to recognize that if the behavior is okay with Jackie and Barbara and Hillary and company, then we've got no cause to bitch.

Hey, Clinton copped to smoking that joint (although I could have done without the questionable inhaling crap, but maybe he'll cop to that one day too). He copped to Gennifer Flowers, and the Republicans may even find something for him to cop to in Whitewater or his campaign-financing mess. And we'll make him cop to every last piece of indecision or cowardice or bad judgment, and in the end what will count is whether or not we think this man has the stones and the heart and the mind to lead this country in a positive direction. Do we believe in what he stands for, and in what he's trying to accomplish? Or do we just want to slap another scarlet letter on yet another person just to help us to feel a little better about ourselves?

Decide, people. Decide.

WIND

We all fart, right? We all get that cramp that tells us there's an air bubble percolating in our butt and it needs to escape. But we don't like to talk about it. Everybody does it, and no one talks about it. Why is that?

Let's break this down. Let's consider the fart in all its wonder. The public fart is a very tricky thing. It's all tied up in where you are, and who you are, and who you're with, and what you ate for lunch. Most people, when they feel a fart coming on, they get up and make for the door, because they're not always sure what that little cramp is telling them. It could be a fart, or it could be one of those power dumps disguised as a fart. Have you ever had one of those? You go to let the air out a little bit and you're surprised by the actual materials you've deposited in your pants. Public farts are troubling enough, but these surprise power dumps are especially upsetting.

For the most part, a fart is a fart. We feel it coming. We know what it is. And we usually have enough butt control to drop 'em at will, or hold 'em back for a more appropriate time, or ease 'em out slow and silent. The game is in figuring out which approach to take, and then what to do with yourself after you've made your deposit.

I'm a great believer in claiming farts. Always have, always will. I don't want to be blamed for one of yours. Mine I know. Mine I can control. Yours, who the fuck knows what's going on down there?

I think there should be some sort of code word, some way to politely signal that you've got some business going on. It's common courtesy. I always call my farts tree monkeys, 'cause tree monkeys make the same farty sound as I do. It's a funny little sound. It would almost be cute, if it wasn't followed by the smell. It's like lightning and thunder. You get that funny little sound, and then the smell hits you. Sometimes it takes a few beats; sometimes it hits you right away. I just say, "Tree monkey," then I get up and walk away. I don't wait for it to hit. I go to the

other end of the room and let people
figure it out for themselves.

I love folks who say, "No, no, mine
don't smell. I just farted, but it doesn't
have any odor." Maybe to you, pinhead, but it
stinks like shit to me. Some people actually
enjoy the smell of their own farts, and that's
fine if they do their farting at home, but when
they take 'em out on tour they need to know.
Mine, of course, are the exception to this rule.
Mine aren't too bad, and this is not just my
opinion. I've had corroboration on the violet
scent of my behind. I should probably bottle it,
and call it *Whoopi*. *Essence of Whoopi*, from
Prince Matchabelli, you know.

Elevators are a problem. There should be
some scanning device built into all new elevators that lets people know if there's a fart on
board. Old elevators should be retired to
accommodate the new ones. This would just be
another common courtesy. Maybe there could
be a big sign (FART ENCLOSED!) to warn people away. You have to know what you're deal-
ing with before you step inside, because being
trapped in an elevator with someone else's fart
is one of the worst fates known to modern
man. There's nothing you can do about it, and
people have a right to know what to expect.
The odor is bad enough, but there's also
the responsibility. Somebody else always
gets on the elevator and thinks it's yours,

and you want to say, "No, no, no. This was here when I arrived. I have nothing to do with what this elevator cab smells like." But you can't say anything. If you say anything, they'll *know* it was you, or maybe they'll just *think* it was you, which pretty much amounts to the same thing. We're all so tense about our farts, and accounting for our farts. We can't even hold up a little yellow piece of notepaper that says, "This is not mine. This belongs to somebody else."

My mother had a great expression, "More room out than in," which basically meant, you know, that there's more room outside your body for this little air bubble than there is inside. More room out than in. It was a sweet little phrase, and it reminded me that farting is a natural thing. Holding on to it is unnatural, and it can lead to all sorts of problems. Ulcers. Gastrointestinal problems. A lot of those plumbing complications that hit us when we get older are caused or aggravated by holding on to your farts, so you've got to let fly.

I've had serious ulcers for years and years, and I'm now the fart queen, the ruler of all I pollute. If I'm not dropping air biscuits, something's wrong. A lot of people don't know this about me, and until now I've been refined enough to keep it to myself, but that's how I got my name, from my frequent

farting. When I was in my twenties
and diagnosed with ulcers, I was
encouraged to fart up a storm, and
my friends started calling me
Whoopi. I was like a walking whoopee cush-
ion, they said. It was an easy tag, and the name
stuck. The name lingers, like a good fart, long
after my violet scent has dissipated.

So it's a very healthy thing to do, and it's an
unavoidable thing to do, and we should all just
ease up a bit about it. There should be some
basic rules, but we shouldn't go holding back
and making ourselves sick. Yeah, there's more
room out than in, but sometimes the outside
environment is just not ready for you. People
shouldn't be allowed to fart if they're standing
on a crowded bus or subway, because their
butt's in someone's face and it's just too lethal;
it's a direct hit, and there's nowhere for the vic-
tim to turn. You shouldn't be allowed to fart on
an airplane, because you can't exactly crack a
window for relief. (Maybe, on international
flights, they should set aside a few rows for
farting.) And you shouldn't be allowed to drop
one of those silent killers and not claim it,
because those SBDs can indeed be deadly.
Some farts should just have people's names on
them, you know.

People have all kinds of techniques to
avoid being found out. Some people keep

pets around, so they can blame their farts on the cat. (Honey, cat farts bleach wood, they're so powerful.)

Some genteel folks lift up one butt cheek, like a dog lifting his leg to pee, to allow the released air a clean path, but I don't understand this move. Do they think the fart won't find their clothes if they're not sitting down? Do they think it won't snake its way into the upholstery? They must think they're liberating the fart and sparing all the fabric in the room.

Some shy folks just hang in there quietly, not saying anything at all, hoping no one will notice, but these people are always an easy mark. When some wicked cheese hits you full in the face, they're the ones with the blank looks, like they don't know what's going on. How can they not know what's going on? It's obvious. *Whoever smelt it, dealt it.* That was a line from my childhood, but it was bullshit. Whoever *didn't* smell it was usually the dealer.

Fart strategy can be tricky. If you're at a party, or a meeting, and you have to drop a little biscuit, do you drop and sit or do you drop and cross the room? Does the smell go with you, or does it stay behind? To the best of my figuring, you're nailed either way, so it's probably better to stay where you are and let the seat cushions absorb the brunt of it. If you move around, you take it with you, and it's like leaving another fart on the other side of the room. There's no sense compounding the problem with a secondhand fart. If you're too chicken- enshit to cop to it, don't get up. Wait it out. And remember, just because you're sit- tin' on it doesn't mean it's not gonna snake its way up and around you. It's gas, and it will come up through your thighs, and people are gonna know it's you anyway. But if you just keep on talking, then suddenly stop and look around to see where that mystery smell came from, that could add to the effect.

The stage gives a great perspective on farts and farting. You look out across those lights, and you can just see the farts on people's faces. The smells don't always find you, all the way up on the stage, but those facial expressions make it plain. In a Broadway house, a lot of the people hurry through a pretheater dinner to make the curtain, and they all bring their farts with them. You'll see someone's eyes pop out, really big, like in one of Rodney Dangerfield's double takes. Or you'll see people squirming in their seats, all crinkled up, like they're trying to hold something back. And then you'll see the people looking around in desperation. They've got their noses pointed up, scoping out some clean air. And you can almost see the gas float from one row to the next, like in a Pepe Le Pew cartoon. The people just fall like

Whoopi Goldberg

dominoes. I always look for the person who's sitting up straight, pretending he doesn't smell anything. He's almost always the culprit, because the key to dropping a fart is you have to smell it too. You have to look as indignant as everyone else. You can't protest too much, in case they trace it back to you, but you've got to protest a little. You've got to go through the motions.

Among the cast and crew, there's a whole farting convention. When I was in *Forum*, on Broadway, there were several noted farters onstage, and there was all kinds of running around in the show, so a lot of times the fartee discovered the fart before the farter was even aware of it. When you're moving around like that, you don't always know. You leave a little trail. Stuff happens. You leave it so people run through your farts when they're crossing the stage. It's like hitting a wall, and they're breathing hard so they've already inhaled it. It's in their lungs.

After a while, you start to recognize each other by the smells you leave behind. Oh, that's Corey. And that one there, that's Whoopi. You just look over at someone and think, That's from your ass, I can tell. You also start to recognize what people have been eating, because certain foods make you fart in certain ways. Beans don't get me the way they get other people. Processed

26

meat always does me in. Deli sand-
wiches are my fiercest enemy when
I'm doing a show, 'cause that lun-
cheon meat makes me very chatty.
Chocolate too. I tend to stay away from chocolate if I'm gonna be out and about. And it's not
just food that determines the tone and tenor of
my anal conversation. When I'm on antibiotics,
I can empty a building. Very few medications
agree with me, but antibiotics yield the most
stunning brew. I'm surprised I've never been
arrested, or committed, for some of the smells
that have come out of me when I'm taking
medicine.

Relationship farts are a whole other deal. The
goal here is to contain yourself until you've
gotten past the I-don't-want-to-take-a-dump-
in-your-bathroom-because-I-don't-want-you-
to-know-my-shit-stinks phase. Once you can
stink up his toilet, you can let fly with
impunity, and you want to get to this place
fairly soon in a relationship because you don't
want to misrepresent yourself to the other person. Love me, love my farts. Love me, and
know that periodically you're gonna open the
bathroom door and get killed.

I resent under-the-cover farts. They're just
not fair. I'm not talking about sex farts.
I've never experienced those, at least not
during the act itself. After you've done the   27

deed, you're up and you're loose and sometimes you let one go, and when that happens it's kinda funny. It's animalistic, but it's playful and it's okay. During the night, though, when I'm sleeping, it's just not fair. It's also animalistic, but it seems to involve only *dead* animals. I'm sorry, but some of those sleep farts wake you in the middle of the night and you think to yourself, What crawled up his ass and died? It's a powerful visual, but really the best way to describe how some of these things can smell.

Ultimately, little kids have got the best handle on this farting business. They've got all kinds of great names and games for it. They pull each other's finger. They light each other's farts. They fart out the alphabet, on cue, or they belt out a cute marching tune. They're proud of their farts and what they can do with them. The louder and wetter and smellier the better. I sometimes try to imagine what the world would be like if we were more like kids in this way. God knows, our elevator rides would never be the same. The cars would be so thick with fart gas we couldn't see our way to the buttons. At work, we'd punctuate our presentations at both ends. We'd fart in each other's faces, and laugh and laugh, and it would be a good thing to give off such a foul smell that it turns someone's skin a different color. Guys with the best farting skills would get all the babes, and we'd be farting up a storm and feeling good about ourselves all over again, for no reason at all.

HEAD

I live with a wonderful man. I've lived with other men in my life too, and not a single one of them has had a clue what he was doing in the bathroom. Not a clue. I don't care how wonderful or presumably wonderful a man is. Surround his ass with tile and porcelain and his head explodes.

I'll tell you what: It doesn't matter how big the damn sink is. A man can't shave or wash without splashing water all over the place. You'd think after all that time standing in front of the sink looking in the mirror, he'd have some idea where to find his face, but from the way he splashes, it's clear he's just hoping to hit his target once in a while. He'll settle for that. They throw the water all over

33

their heads, but they're not shaving their heads. Why does there have to be water everywhere? And why can't they shave in the shower? Haven't they seen those shower mirrors in the hardware store? They're available, you know they're available, so just pick your ass up, go down to the store, and start shaving in the fucking shower.

To most men, this is a ridiculous proposition. They would sooner sing on the subway than shave in the shower. They don't see the need. They just splash all that water around and figure it'll dry up eventually, and it *will* dry up eventually, except that I'm gonna be using that bathroom long before eventually. I have to add five minutes to my routine just to blot down the mess. It gets to where I'm cleaning the bathroom every time I go in there. And then, when you start moving stuff around, you see it's all moldy underneath from all that water, and the little cleanup turns into a giant production. It starts to take all day just to go in and brush out your hair—not that I have much call to brush out my hair. And you can't talk to him about it, because you just can't. You bring it up and a fight begins:

"You're not letting me be myself."

"What do you mean, I'm not letting you be yourself? I'm living with you. I'm sharing a bathroom with you. What the fuck

does the way you splash water
around when you shave have to do
with being yourself?"

"Well, you're coming in anyway.
You're gonna use the sink anyway. It's just
gonna get all wet again, so what's the point?"

"The point is, I don't want to wipe up your
mess, day after day. You made the mess. Wipe
it up!"

And it's not just water. If it was just water,
maybe I could deal. But there's hair, and dried-
up toothpaste spit, and gobs of mucus, and
beard stubble, and little pee spots all over the
seat and floor, and who knows what else? Who
wants to come in and look at that? Who wants
to touch it? It's enough of an ordeal to touch
my own mess, but touching someone else's . . .
Yecchhhh! Please!

Now, this shit doesn't happen at the beginning of a relationship, because that's the oh-
baby-you're-so-wonderful period. That's when
they get you. No one wants to be found out
during the oh-baby period. Men chew their
food before they talk, they don't leave their
crusty underwear on the floor, they don't piss
in the sink. Yes, men actually piss in the sink.
Not right away, but they get to it. Apparently
it's a great burden to them to walk those extra
five feet to the toilet, so they go in the sink.
At first, you have some idea this has been
going on, because like I said, their aim is   35

off, especially late at night. But then you catch them at it and call them on it.

"What the fuck are you doing? I have to use that sink. I soak my panty hose in that sink. I close the drain and fill it up with water and use it to wash my face. What's wrong with you? You don't pee in your mother's sink."

"Just rinse it out," he'll say.

Just rinse it out? Yeah, like that'll cover it. You know, come on. Just come on. Hand me the Lysol and stop peeing in the sink.

And when you've been together long enough, he'll just go in the sink right in front of you. There's no pretense. You'll be using the toilet and he just can't wait. He's got to go. He has to pee in the sink. There's got to be something to this, something primal. Maybe it's a marking-territory kind of thing, to keep the enemies at bay. Maybe it's a fraternity thing, because frat boys just have no sense of how to behave when it comes to their bodily functions; they could be eighty years old and still think it's a hoot to leave a lit bag of shit on someone's doorstep.

The pissing in the sink is bad enough, but there's other stuff. As the days go by, there are more spots around the tub, or on the floor. The shower isn't rinsed out, there are pubic hairs on the soap, the bathtub has a ridge of scum around it. This is the wake-up period when you realize you're deep into the same old shit. The oh-baby period is over and you've been had. You think to yourself, Where am I? Who is this person I moved in with? When will I learn?

I'm just as bad, I suppose. We women have got our own weird behaviors. Me, I have lotions. All over the place, I have lotions. Moisturizers, remoisturizers, post-moisturizers, every damn cream you can find, meant to do every damn thing to your skin. You make it, I'll buy it, and then I'll line it up in my bathroom and arrange it in sequence with all the others. Then I have my different soaps, because one day I'll want to smell like peppermint and one day I'll want to smell like almonds and one day I'll want to be all tutti-frutti. I'll have eight or nine going at the same time. And you can't have just one shampoo. You've got to have the shampoo that feeds the hair, the shampoo for when your scalp is dry, the shampoo that deals with split ends, the shampoo that adds luster. (Because, darling, you can never have too much luster.)

He'll look at all my creams and shit and wonder what I'm doing. I can see that, I guess. I can see how all my lotions and soaps and shampoos would freak a guy out, especially when I won't let him touch any of it or move the stuff around. I use them all in order. I start with this and then I do this and then I do this. The sequence is key. I don't want no guy coming in and messing with my sequence.

Finally, when we've each pretty much had it with the other person, one of us will suggest we have separate bathrooms. This is the desperation period, because most people can't afford separate bathrooms. It's not practical. Even if you can afford it, who's gonna be the one to have to walk down the hall to use the bathroom at the other end of the house? Who wants to pee in Siberia?

Most people probably don't want separate bathrooms, deep down. It runs counter to the notions of partnership and sharing and commitment behind most relationships. Once you're living together, separate bathrooms are one step away from separate bedrooms, or maybe those separate twin beds, like Rob and Laura Petrie used to have.

So the thing to do is get along. Or try. Figure out what kinds of things come out of and go into each other's bodies, or on each other's skin. Ladies, know that your man is gonna miss the toilet from time to time, or splash water around while he's shaving, or leave his pubic hairs on the soap. Learn to adjust. And that goes for you men too. Don't get all bent over a box of sanitary napkins.

Once in a while, we're gonna leave them out for a few days, 'cause it's easier than ducking into that cupboard underneath the wet sink every time we need one. And we've got a whole assortment: different sizes for the underpants of the day, others for heavy days, and others for light days . . . we're just trying to cover all the bases.

And while we're on the subject, why is it that no man wants to hear about your period? They say, "Oh, you got your period?" Then they leave the room. Maybe they want us to go off in the woods for a few days and get it over with. They think we bleed like we've been shot, and they think we're gonna be all cranky.

Well, yeah, sometimes we get cranky. Just deal with it. Part of it is hormonal, but part of it is just being reminded that we have to deal with it ourselves. Every month we have to deal with it. And part of it is just tactical. The stuff they sell us to absorb the flow of menstrual blood doesn't always work the way it's supposed to. Sometimes, you bleed right through your clothes and people notice and move away from you and point you out to their children. Sometimes, with the glue they've got now at the bottom of these sanitary napkins, you can step the wrong way and glue yourself down. Let me tell you, there's nothing worse than walking down the street, doing your "Charlie" bounce, or your *That Girl* slide, swinging your bag, swinging your hair, and then one of your pubes gets caught in that sticky stuff. Your eyes well up, you can't move, you just turn cold and then hot. And it's not like we allow each other to scratch our butts in public. You can't stop to scratch or adjust yourself. You can't just turn to the guy next to you and smile sheepishly and say, "Oh, dear, my pubes are stuck." You've just got to reach in there and do what you have to do and hope no one you know is watching.

Tampons are a different bother. They're almost never moisturized, which means they've got to go in with kind of a push, and it hurts like hell, and as many men can tell you, it's probably no picnic for the tampon either; you need a little lubrication. And then you have to squat, or straddle the bowl if you're in a public rest room, and fiddle with the cardboard and the string and do the best you can, but the best you can still leaves you with a little string dangling from your vagina. I don't know about you, but I walk around feeling like one of those wooden marionettes. You know, pull my string and my arms'll flap up and down. It's just too fucking ridiculous.